Making a R

Frances Ridley

OXFORD
UNIVERSITY PRESS

These machines make roads.

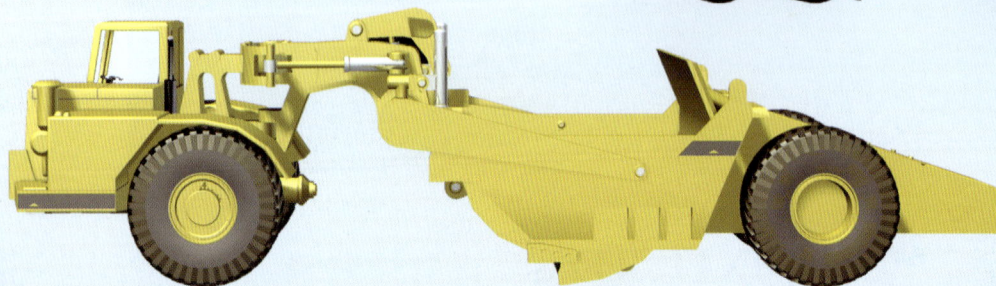

All the machines have a job to do.

This machine makes a track for the road.

bulldozer

earth

This machine makes a hole for the pipes.

excavator

pipes

This machine makes the track flat.

The road will go here.

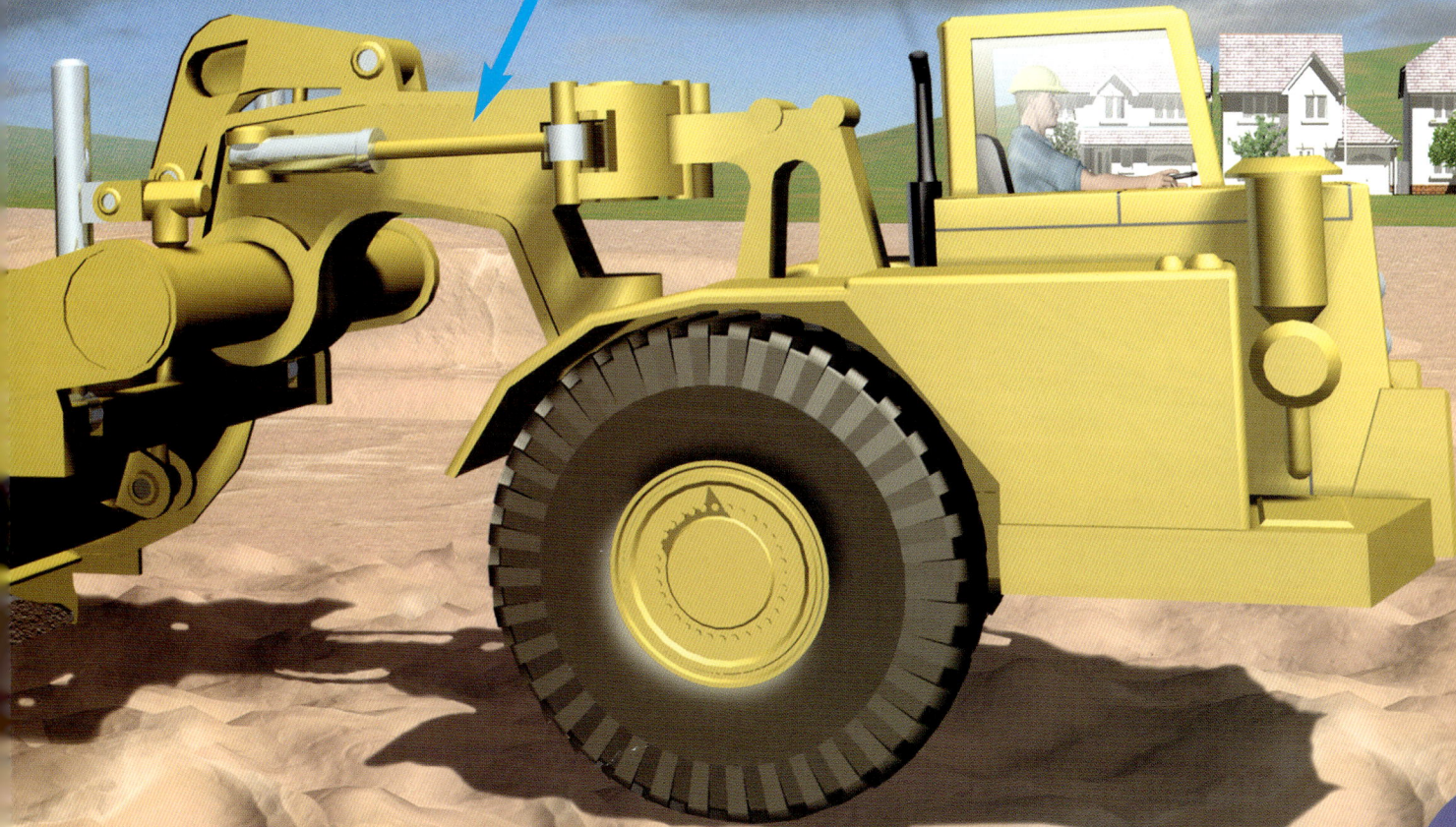

grader

This big truck takes the earth away.

excavator

dumper truck

More trucks bring big stones.
They tip the stones over
the road.

This machine rolls over the stones. It makes them flat.

road roller

This truck brings small stones and tar.

small stones and tar

truck

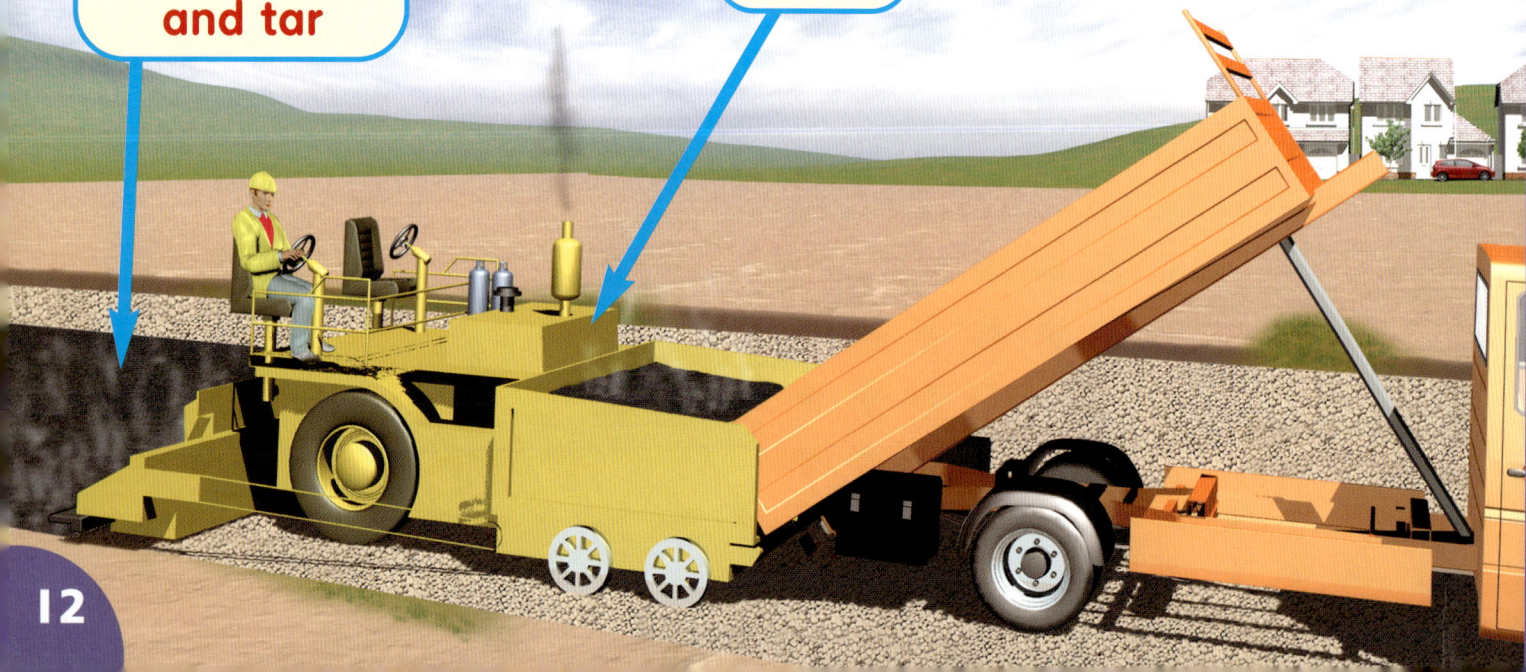

This machine puts the stones and tar all over the road.

small stones and tar

paver

This machine rolls over the road. It makes the road flat.

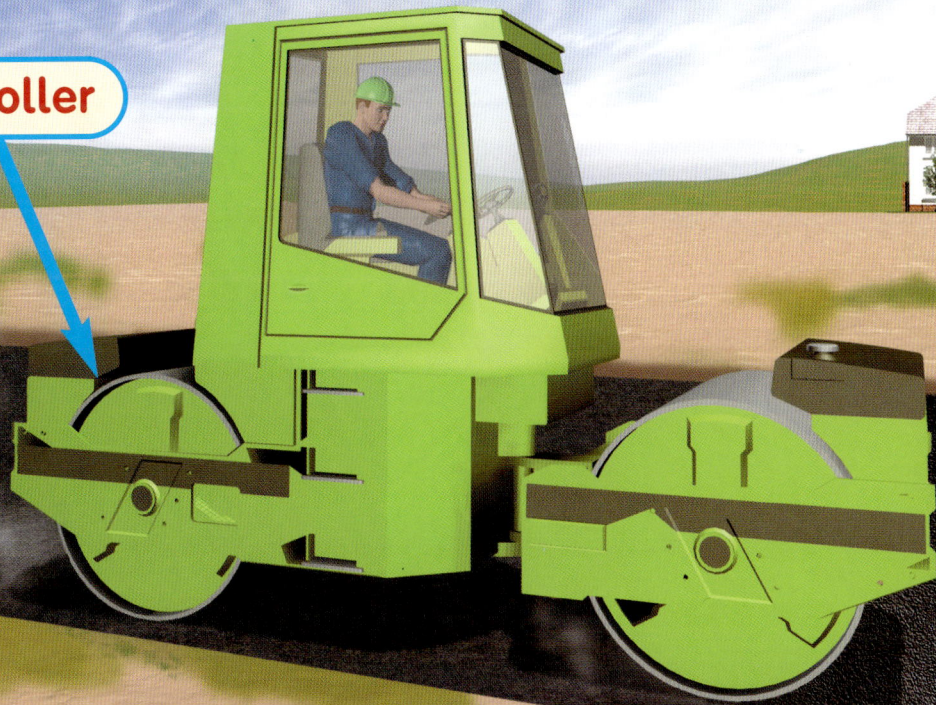

road roller

The road needs lights...

cherry picker

...and painted lines.

pram

15

Now the road is ready. Here come the cars!